Watch It Grow

Frog

Barrie Watts

Smart Apple Media

First published in 2003 by Franklin Watts
96 Leonard Street, London EC2A 4XD, United Kingdom
Franklin Watts Australia, 56 O'Riordan Street, Alexandria, NSW 2015
Copyright © 2003 Barrie Watts

Editor: Jackie Hamley, Art director: Jonathan Hair, Photographer: Barrie
Watts, Illustrator: David Burroughs, Reading consultant: Beverley Mathias

Published in the United States by Smart Apple Media
1980 Lookout Drive, North Mankato, Minnesota 56003

U.S. publication copyright © 2004 Smart Apple Media
International copyright reserved in all countries. No part of this book may
be reproduced in any form without written permission from the publisher.
Printed in Hong Kong

Library of Congress Cataloging-in-Publication Data

Watts, Barrie. Frog / Barrie Watts. p. cm. — (Watch it grow)
Summary: A simple introduction to the physical characteristics
and behavior of frogs, emphasizing their development from the
day they hatch until they lay eggs of their own.
ISBN 1-58340-233-0 1. Frogs—Life cycles—Juvenile literature.
[1. Frogs.] I. Title.
QL668.E2W33 2003 597.8'9—dc21 2003042515

2 4 6 8 9 7 5 3 1

How to use this book

Watch It Grow has been specially designed to cater to a range of reading and learning abilities. Initially children may just follow the pictures. Ask them to describe in their own words what they see. Other children will enjoy reading the single sentence in large type in conjunction with the pictures. This single sentence is then expanded in the main text. More adept readers will be able to follow the text and pictures by themselves through to the conclusion of the frog's life cycle.

Contents

Frogs come from eggs.

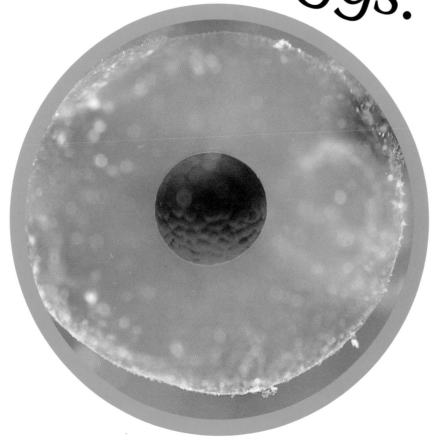

Here is an egg laid by a female frog. The egg is surrounded by a ball of jelly. Together, the egg and jelly are about the size of a pea. The jelly is tough and protects the dark egg in the middle.

A female frog lays hundreds of eggs at one time. She lays them in a pond or marsh. The eggs are all stuck together in a big lump called **frogspawn**.

The egg changes.

After a week, the dark egg in the
middle of the jelly begins to
change shape. It slowly becomes
a soft, wriggling creature about
as long as a grain of rice.

A baby frog, called a **tadpole**, is growing. The **tadpole** eats food stored in the egg. After about two weeks, all the food in the egg has been used up, and the jelly around it has become softer.

The tadpole hatches.

When the **tadpole** is ready to hatch, it wriggles through the soft jelly. The **tadpole** has a large head and tail. It will use its tail for swimming.

For the first few days after hatching, the **tadpole** rests. It uses a small sucker on its chin to stick to the rest of the **frogspawn** or a plant.

The tadpole breathes underwater.

In order to live, the **tadpole** needs to breathe. It has to take **oxygen** from the water. The **tadpole** breathes by using two feathery limbs called **gills**. There is one gill on each side of its head. The **gills** take **oxygen** from the water and pass it to the **tadpole's** blood.

The **tadpole** also needs to find food. It feeds on tiny green plants called **algae**, which grow on waterweeds.

The tadpole's body changes.

After about six weeks, the **tadpole** starts to grow back legs. The **tadpole** is getting bigger. It now eats larger foods such as small water worms.

The feathery **gills** by its head have disappeared, and the **tadpole** now breathes using **gills** inside its body. It sucks in water through its mouth. It then pushes the water over the **gills** and out a breathing hole called a **spiracle**.

spiracle

The front legs grow.

Four weeks later, the **tadpole** begins to grow its front legs. At first the legs look like flaps of skin. Each day they grow longer. Soon they look like a pair of legs with clawed feet on the ends.

The **tadpole's** mouth and eyes are getting bigger, and its tail is slowly shrinking. The **tadpole** is beginning to look like a frog.

The tadpole uses its lungs.

When the **tadpole's** front legs grow, they close up the **spiracle**. This means that the **tadpole** can no longer use the **gills** inside its body. Instead, it starts to take **oxygen** from the air.

Now the **tadpole** begins to use its **lungs**. It swims to the surface of the water to breathe in air. The **tadpole** had **lungs** when it hatched, but they were too small to use at first.

The frog comes out of the water.

After 12 weeks, the **tadpole** has turned into a small frog. Its tail has become much smaller, so it uses its legs to swim.

The frog now spends more time
out of the water. It sits on lily
pads and floating weeds, or by
the side of the pond, looking for
small insects to eat.

The frog can jump.

A small frog makes a tasty meal for **predators**. A frog's **predators** include cats and birds. If the frog senses **predators** nearby, it jumps into the water for safety.

The frog's strong back legs are like springs. It uses them to leap up to 10 times its body length, especially when it is young and not too heavy.

The frog looks for food.

It will take two years for the young frog to become an adult. The frog now spends most of its time on land. It hides under a rock or log during the day. At night, it comes out to look for food.

The frog tries to eat any moving creature that is smaller than itself. It especially likes worms. The frog cleans the soil from the worms by pulling them through its front claws. Then it swallows them whole.

The frog sleeps through the winter.

In late fall, frogs **hibernate**. They sleep through the winter to survive the cold. During their long sleep, they live on food they have stored in their bodies.

Female frogs and young frogs usually hide in a damp place on land to **hibernate**. Adult male frogs usually sleep hidden in mud at the bottom of a pond. There they breathe through their skin.

The frog looks for a pond.

In early spring, the female frogs wake up and search for a pond. They always look for the pond they grew up in. They can tell which is the right pond by the smell of the water.

Sometimes frogs travel a long way looking for the right pond, crossing roads, rivers, and other ponds until they find it.

The female frog lays her eggs.

After **hibernation**, the female frog looks fat. Her body is full of eggs. When she arrives at the right pond, the male frogs are already waiting. The female chooses a male frog with whom to mate.

The male frog clings to her back. As she lays her eggs, he **fertilizes** them. The female frog then leaves the pond and will not come back until next year. The eggs are left to hatch on their own. Soon, **tadpoles** begin to wriggle inside the **frogspawn**.

Word bank

Algae - moss-like plants that grow in water or damp places. Tadpoles eat algae.

Fertilizes - when male sperm meets a female egg, the egg is fertilized, and a new life is formed. Male frogs squirt sperm onto the female's eggs to fertilize them.

Frogspawn - a lump of frog eggs stuck together.

Gills - parts of the body used to take oxygen from the water. Tadpoles have two different kinds of gills.

Hibernate, Hibernation - when an animal hides and goes into a deep sleep during the cold winter.

Lungs - bag-like organs inside an animal's body that are used to breathe air.

Oxygen - a gas found in air and water. Animals must breathe it to live.

Predators - animals that hunt and eat other animals.

Spiracle - a breathing hole. A whale's blowhole is a spiracle. Tadpoles use a spiracle when they breathe through the gills inside their bodies.

Tadpole - the young, fish-like form of a frog or toad before it becomes an adult.

Life cycle

 A week after being laid, the frog egg starts to change into a tadpole.

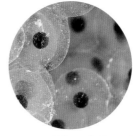 The following spring, the female frog lays her eggs.

 About a week later, the tadpole hatches. It soon eats algae and breathes using gills outside its body.

 The young frog hibernates. After two years, the frog is fully grown and ready to mate.

 Six weeks after hatching, the tadpole starts to grow back legs. It now breathes through its spiracle.

 Twelve weeks after hatching, the tadpole has become a small frog. Its tail is smaller, and its eyes are bigger.

Four weeks later, the tadpole starts to grow front legs.

As the front legs grow, the tadpole starts breathing through its lungs.

Index